Me and Fundamentalists

Encounters and Observations

Paul W. Bass and Bob Perry

With Foreword by Dr. Bob Dale

Published, 2020
By Amazon/Kindle

Me and Fundamentalists

Table of Contents

Foreword..5
Introduction..7
About the Authors...9

Chapter One:
Early Personal Awareness of Fundamentalists..........17

Chapter Two:
Growing Presence of Fundamentalists.......................27

Chapter Three:
Dominant Presence of Fundamentalists.....................37

Chapter Four:
Practices of Fundamentalists.......................................47

Chapter Five:
Dangers of Fundamentalists..53

Chapter Six:
Future of Fundamentalists...57

Conclusion..61

Addendum:
Fundamentalists in the Scriptures and History..........65

Afterword..69

Authors' Publications..71

Research and Resources..73

Acknowledgments...75

Me and Fundamentalists

Foreword

Each of us has a special faith story to tell. My faith pilgrimage, as a native of Southwest Missouri, is a lot like the journeys of Paul and Bob. I grew up so totally Baptist that I never spoke to a Catholic or Jewish person, to an African or an Asian person until I enrolled in the University of Missouri.

My world got much bigger when I wrote my doctoral dissertation on 20th century Baptists --- Walter Rauschenbusch, John R. Rice, Carl F. H. Henry, and Harvey Cox. My research began with a study of *The Fundamentals: A Testimony to the Truth*, a series of twelve pamphlets that confronted "modernist" theology and were released between 1910-1915. Then, I later lived through the Baptist battles.

Read and ponder and learn from Paul and Bob's stories. Let your faith story mature too!

   ---**Bob Dale, PhD**, Richmond, VA
   Author, Professor, Pastor, Consultant, Executive Coach

Me and Fundamentalists

Introduction

It is important to state at the beginning that we do not hate fundamentalists or fundamentalism. Fundamentalists are our brothers in Christ. We hate what some radical fundamentalists have done that has affected, friends, churches, schools and denominations.

It is important that we begin with a definition of "fundamental." It is defined as "serving as, or being an essential part of, a foundation or basis, basic, underlying." It is interesting to note the changing status of "fundamental" in the actions of Baptist fundamentalists. In 1963, Baptists saw the new Baptist Faith and Message as a basic understanding of who we were as Baptists. In 2000, fundamentalist leadership in control of the Southern Baptist Convention expanded the basics to a new Baptist Faith and Message, more clearly understood as a creedal statement. For many members of Baptist education and denominational organizations, even further expansions of acceptable beliefs were added over the next two decades. The idea of "fundamental" basics has been greatly expanded that excluded many valuable participants in the SBC and state conventions.

Our intent in this book is to share our experiences with the impacts of these radical elements in our past and present and to express concerns on the future effect of their actions. Every attempt has been made to provide accurate historical data for the events described.

It is also important to declare that the results of these actions are our personal interpretations. We acknowledge the right to be wrong, but also acknowledge the right to be right.

Why are we writing this book? First, to help us understand our own pilgrimage in faith to where we are today. Second, is to help others understand and process their similar pilgrimages of faith. Third, is to offer speculation into the future of where our faith is heading in relation to fellow believers, churches, schools and denominations. Last, we hope that this book will help us to look beyond the temporal, imperfect work of God's kingdom on earth to the eternal, perfect purpose of God's work through His people in our nation and beyond.

Me and Fundamentalists

Authors' Backgrounds

It is very important for the reader to know our backgrounds and experiences. These have provided the basis for our observations about experiences with fundamentalism in churches, Christian schools and denominational organizations.

Paul Bass
Family:

I grew up in Independence, Missouri as the oldest of six boys. My parents had no commitment to any church or religious affiliation. My mother's family were members in the Reorganized Latter Day Saints church. My experience with the Baptist Church began as an invitation to attend a summer Vacation Bible School program at the nearby Beverly Hills Baptist Church. It was a two-week event from early morning until noon. From that experience I was invited to their Sunday School program. I enjoyed the junior department activities and my junior department class. Floyd Kelly was my teacher. He was a very nice man that we liked, but we were often not very cooperative in class.

One Sunday morning I began to ask a lot of questions about my relationship with God. Mr. Kelly listened attentively and we talked after class. He shared the story of Jesus' love for me and I prayed to receive Christ in that basement classroom. I shared my profession of faith with the church that morning. Our pastor visited with my parents about baptism and church membership. My parents were somewhat suspicious and asked that I wait for a year to be baptized to ensure that this was not a short-term experience.

I began to participate in other church activities such as Royal Ambassadors and Church Training. I enjoyed the social activities provided for the church's growing children and youth. When I was eleven years old, my parents allowed me to be baptized along with a younger brother. I became an active member of the Beverly Hills Baptist Church.

Education:
My grade school experiences began at Spring Branch Elementary School for the first grade. At Alton Elementary school, I attended second through sixth grades. At Independence Junior High School, I completed seventh through eighth grades. I completed William Chrisman High School, graduating in 1964. Our graduation was held at the world headquarters of the Reorganized Latter Day Saints.

In the summer of 1964, I left home for Southwest Baptist College in Bolivar, Missouri. My Associate of Arts and Bachelor of Arts degrees were completed in 1966 and 1968 respectively. In the fall of 1965, after praying with my dorm mates, I felt a strong call to the gospel ministry. I shared that with my home church and received a license to preach the gospel.

In 1968, I enrolled at Midwestern Baptist Theological Seminary in Kansas City, Missouri. The seminary was dually accredited with North Central Accrediting as well as seminary accreditation. I married Jan Smashey on June 15, 1969 in the Southern Hills Baptist Church in Bolivar. I graduated from seminary in 1971 with a Masters in Religious Education.

Professionalism:
My last year at Midwestern Seminary, I was fortunate to work with Dr. John Howell in establishing the Northside Baptist Church in Gladstone, Missouri. My responsibilities were in youth, education and music. Just before graduation, I was ordained to the gospel ministry by Beverly Hills Baptist Church.

For the next nineteen years, I worked in full time church staff positions in Arkansas, Alabama and Missouri. Work was in youth, education, associate pastoring and pastoring. There was enjoyment working with the state conventions in leading associational and state training conferences. There were also opportunities to lead in summer mission trips for youth and adults. Camp and retreat programs were also conducted.

In 1990, I was asked to consider serving as Student Activities Director at Ouachita Baptist University in Arkadelphia, Arkansas. I began serving in that role in the fall of 1990. That position offered opportunities for adjunct teaching, supply preaching, interim pastorates and a bi-vocational pastorate. I participated in the Ministry Inservice Guidance program of the Southern Baptist Education Commission. When the commission was eliminated by convention leaders, I helped preserve the historical materials in four file cabinets located in the library at Baylor University in Waco, Texas.

I was also the debate coach for the International Public Debate Association team at Ouachita Baptist University. We won several national championships and scholarly debate was a real joy.

In 2007, I accepted an early retirement program offered by the university. I was asked to continue some limited adjunct teaching for the next few years. I had begun to enjoy research and writing of several books. In 2011, we bought a retirement house in Willard, Missouri. I moved there while Jan stayed in Arkadelphia to complete her work. After much commuting for over a year, we both settled in Willard. I continued research and writing historical nonfiction books. I was fortunate to have published nine books by then, winning several awards.

In 2011, we joined University Heights Baptist Church in Springfield, Missouri. It is a dually aligned church with the Cooperative Baptist Fellowship and American Baptist Churches. It left the Missouri Baptist Convention because of their new membership demands, but remained active in the Greene County Baptist Association. I have been privileged to supply preach in several churches and teach an adult Sunday School class.

I have been able to publish twelve books, with four receiving awards and recognitions. I have traveled throughout the state in book promotional events. I was asked to teach Bible classes at Mercy School of Nursing at Springfield, Missouri, through a cooperative degree program with Southwest Baptist University. The threats of fundamentalist takeover became very personal when the Missouri Baptist Convention asserted its control of the Board of Trustees for SBU in the fall of 2019. It became personal because of family members employed at SBU and the threat of their future there. It is also personal because of my appreciation for the new president, Dr. Eric Turner. It is also personal because it is my alma mater.

I hope that the understanding of my background and experiences gives me some credibility in writing about the experiences with fundamentalism in churches, Christian schools and denominational organizations. It is my hope that as many others have shared similar personal experiences, we can become more involved and prayerful about family and friends caught in this needless web of political power efforts under the smokescreen of doctrinal purity.

Bob Perry

Family:
My parents, Bob L. Perry and Lena M. Smith grew up in Marionville, MO, and were married in January of 1944 while Dad was on a short furlough from the US Army. He was then transferred to a base in California, where Mom accompanied him. Later he shipped off to the war in Europe, serving primarily in Sicily and Italy. I was born in January of 1945 while he was in the middle of his war experience.

I lived my first four years in Aurora, MO; then my folks bought an 80 acre farm near Verona, MO. Mom and Dad were both very active in First Baptist, Aurora and then at Verona Baptist. At one time or another they held most every lay position available in a Baptist church. We were there Sunday morning, Sunday night, Wednesday night, every revival meeting- attendees that pastors loved.

I had a sister four years younger, and eventually my parents had the wonderful surprise of another little girl born the year I left home for college. I adored my two sisters, though I was not always nice to the one I grew up with. At the age of nine, during a decision time in Vacation Bible School, I made my decision to become a follower of Christ, and I was baptized in Spring River shortly thereafter.

I was active in church throughout my childhood and teenage years, though I was also involved in various kinds of mischief at school and with my peers. Dad worked as a carpenter and cabinet maker, as well as tending the farm. My Saturdays were almost always spent shoveling manure from the dairy barn, driving the tractor to plow, plant or harvest the fields, cutting firewood with Dad with a crosscut saw, and building or mending fences.

When I was 15, I took over the milking. Dad let me buy the dairy feed for our small herd of 6 to 8 cows and keep the milk checks. This gave me spending money and let me save for college.

Education:
   Verona School did not have kindergarten, but I was allowed to start first grade when I was five. I was more interested in having fun and being a class clown than learning my lessons. That began to change in fifth grade, when Mrs. Pennell, walking through the class while we were doing a writing assignment, picked up my paper and showed it to the rest of the class. She said, "Look, class, at this good work Bobby has done." It felt so good to get that praise from the teacher that from then on I made A's in everything. I graduated from Verona High School as valedictorian of a class of 20 in 1962; then it was off to college at Southwest Missouri State in Springfield (now Missouri State University). There I became very active in the Baptist Student Union and First Baptist Church of Springfield. After feeling called to the ministry, that church licensed me to the ministry, and I was later ordained at Mt. Zion Baptist Church east of Ozark, MO. Nancy Whitlow and I were married in 1964.
   I graduated from SMS in 1966, with a Bachelor of Science degree and a lifetime teaching certificate for secondary level math. That major was chosen before I felt the call to ministry. I entered Midwestern Baptist Theological Seminary in Kansas City in 1967, and by this time we had a newborn son, Douglas Robert. During seminary years I served as pastor of two different part-time student pastorates in the Kansas City area. I graduated with a Master of Divinity degree in 1970.
   During 1978, while on furlough from the mission field, I began study toward a Doctor of Ministry degree at Midwestern, completing the degree in 1980.

Professionalism:
   After beginning ministry in a small Springfield church as music leader, I became youth minister at Temple Baptist Church in Springfield. From there I went to my first pastorate at Mount Zion at Ozark, MO. Then I was off to seminary.

After graduation from seminary, I was called to be pastor of Pisgah Baptist Church near Excelsior Springs, MO, where our son, David Andrew, was born. After four years at Pisgah, Nancy and I felt called to foreign missions, and were appointed by the Foreign Mission Board of the Southern Baptist Convention to be missionaries to Mexico. We served in Guadalajara, Oaxaca and Mexico City until 1980. Due to some chronic health issues related to water, food and air in Mexico with several of the family, we returned to the US in 1980.

I served as pastor of First Baptist Church at Excelsior Springs, MO from 1980 to 1984, when I was called as director of missions for Clay-Platte Baptist Association in Kansas City, MO. From there I went to be executive director of the Mt. Vernon Baptist Association in Annandale, VA (now North Star Church Network). While there, my wife Nancy, died of melanoma cancer.

I married Dr. Marilyn Christian Nelson in 1993. She was a home missionary and had served for 10 years as the director of Christian social ministries for the D. C. Baptist Convention and director of the Johenning Baptist Center in Anacostia.

In 1993, Marilyn became associate professor of Christian Ministry at the Baptist Theological Seminary in Richmond, VA, and we began 4 years in a commuter marriage, since my work in Northern Virginia was a two-hour drive from Richmond. In 1997, I was called to be executive director of the Richmond Baptist Association, where I served until retirement in 2003.

We chose Springfield, MO as our place of retirement and built a new home on eight acres near Willard, MO. We joined University Heights Baptist Church, which is dually aligned with American Baptist Churches, USA and with the Cooperative Baptist Fellowship (CBF). We continued to work in various part-time capacities. We led a leadership development program for young church leaders for the CBF and CBF of Missouri (now Heartland CBF). I had, by this time written several books on church health and strategic planning, so I served as a church consultant with Churchnet (the Baptist General Convention of Missouri) and the Greene County Baptist Association.

At age 75, I continue to enjoy ministry through my local church, the local association, and a number of volunteer opportunities in the Ozarks. In 2015, I worked through our church to begin a low-interest loan program to help people trapped in predatory payday and title loans. Marilyn and I are able to travel, enjoy our home and enjoy the grandkids.

I appreciate Paul Bass inviting me to join him in this writing project. If this were a scholarly treatise requiring intensive research, I probably would not be doing it. But as an opportunity to share my personal experience with fundamentalism, including the anger, hurt and disappointment I have felt from it, I welcome the invitation.

Me and Fundamentalists

Chapter One: Early Awareness of Fundamentalists

Paul Bass

Churches/Denomination:

My first experience with fundamentalist behavior occurred in Batesville, Arkansas. I had been pastor of a mission church in 1971 for several years before going to the mother church in Batesville as minister of youth and education. The new mission pastor, a graduate of an in-state Bible College, was welcomed and I spent some time helping him adjust to the mission field. Before long, the mission appealed to the mother church for full church status. I was supportive of the move when the pastor indicated his interest in becoming actively involved in the local associational work. There were rumblings of discontent from some of the mission members about the new pastor's intentions after achieving church status. A meeting was held to discuss the situation.

At the meeting the pastor indicated his intention to establish an Independent Baptist Church. He was critical of the mother church's oversight of the earlier work done in the mission under my leadership. He even went so far as to accuse me of teaching the youth how to gamble, showing the bingo markers used for youth game night as evidence of betting chips. He was caught off guard when informed that the mission constitution stated that the church property would revert to the association should the church become anything other than a Southern Baptist Church.

His actions angered many of those present and he was asked to resign. He did resign and immediately established his own church in the same mission field with several of the mission members he had developed as faithful followers.

I learned early on some of the tactics used by some fundamentalist leaders in lying about their intentions, attacking supposed enemies with false accusations and developing a handful of faithful followers.

Other than an academic knowledge of historic fundamentalism, I cannot recall any other firsthand experiences with the practice before the 1980s. Being able to attend a Southern Baptist Convention meeting in Los Angeles, California, I became aware of the growing political influence of fundamentalists in denominational organization. Friendship with a past president of the convention and contact with other respected denominational leaders, allowed me to recognize their concerns that the actions of this organized political group was no passing fancy.

The well-orchestrated actions of the fundamentalist group enabled them to slowly dominate convention leadership with control of officers and especially the powerful nominating committee. Personnel and policies began to change the traditional practices of convention organizations and committees. Busing in of delegates from fundamentalist churches helped to ensure convention control.

In my personal experiences in churches as a full time staff member I did not encounter direct, local fundamentalist actions. As a bi-vocational pastor in Arkansas, I was challenged to have our church be compliant with the new fundamentalist initiated 2000 Baptist Faith and Message. The church had happily adopted the 1963 Baptist Faith and Message. After explanation of the new creedal aspect of the 2000 Baptist Faith and Message, our church approved continuing to operate with the 1963 Baptist Faith and Message. It did not affect our church's fellowship as it sadly would in many other churches.

I do recall many friends in the Missouri Baptist Convention leadership being forced out or resigning due to the fundamentalist takeover in the late 1980s and early 1990s.

Another personal, but indirect experience, occurred with developments in Southern Hills Baptist Church in Bolivar, Missouri. My wife and I were active members there during our college years. In 1969, we were married there. Our family were active members there. A new pastor with a fundamentalist agenda began to change the church, its organization and its democratic practices. Leaders became "elders". No business could come before the church unless it had been approved by the elders. The church's constitution was changed to support the changes. A strong effort was made to get support of longtime members who had objected to the changes. Members who were not regular attenders of worship services were dismissed. Our family members continued their teaching responsibilities, but began to withdraw from worship services. Their children had left to join another local church.

The elders in the church became very active in the state convention activities and gained responsible positions in the convention committees.

Education:

I do remember one student in my religion classes at SWBC who would occasionally challenge the professor with "Landmarkist" beliefs. It seemed to be a friendly discussion with gracious latitude in sharing beliefs. There had been challenges in the 1950s to a professor at Midwestern Baptist Seminary over teachings in writing about the book of Genesis. This appeared to be a question of doctrinal beliefs absent any organized political action.

It was not until I was at Ouachita Baptist University that I saw firsthand the aggressive and underhanded actions of organized political actions by fundamentalists trying to take over the Arkansas Baptist Convention. In the mid 1990s, efforts were made to influence the Nominating Committee and Finance Committees of the Arkansas Baptist Convention. The goal was to eventually control both committees and attack Ouachita Baptist University. There were false claims of false teaching in the religion department and strong criticism of past and current university presidents.

One year they were able to table the annual state convention financial support of Ouachita pending investigation of charges. They also succeeded in a Nominating Committee report to replace the annual university recommended trustees with their own slate of fundamentalists. The university president announced that Ouachita would return to its original charter calling for the school to replace its own trustees.

During the year, the fundamentalist group met in strategy planning and discussed their ultimate goal of dominating the state convention and recreating Ouachita in their image. Word of their plans leaked out to pastors in the state. At the next convention meeting, the convention overwhelmingly voted to restore the financial support for the university and approve its trustee recommendations. Soundly defeated, the fundamentalists gave up their political takeover attempts. The key leadership of the group moved to England to explore possible control of the English Baptist churches.

After having retired to Willard, Missouri, I was asked to serve as adjunct teacher of Bible classes at SBU's Mercy School of Nursing in Springfield. I became part of the Redford School of Religion. The Missouri Baptist Convention had been involved for nearly two decades in trying to take control of the convention's various organizations. After multiple expensive lawsuits, they won some and lost some. Four of the convention-sponsored schools were under attack for control of trustees and operations.

One prominent school chose to forgo the convention's financial support and control. Two others submitted to the convention demands. In 2018, the fundamentalists found an opening to attack and gain control of Southwest Baptist University. A theology professor, Clint Bass (no relation), at SBU had been meeting secretly with state and Southern

Baptist Convention leaders to gather discrediting information on other SBU faculty and administration. Bass and SBU trustee, Kyle Lee, were serving as elders at Southern Hills Baptist Church in Bolivar, Missouri. Bass had gathered unfounded accusations of heretical teachings of his fellow theology professors through largely indirect, student reports. He never confronted the professors directly about the accusations.

When the SBU administration discovered the secret plot to discredit the theology professors, Bass was called to give account of his actions. He acknowledged his actions with no apology. The SBU board of trustees and the new president, Eric Turner, took action. In November 2018, Bass was fired for violation of the SBU handbook and failure to adhere to biblical procedures regarding confrontation with his fellow believers on faculty. Lee was censured as a trustee and his failure to answer questions about his actions, prompted the trustees to fire him in January 2019.

Lee and Bass maintained continued conversation with state denominational leaders and planned a coup at the October 2019 annual session. The usual practice of accepting a recommended slate of trustees by SBU was rejected by the state nominating committee, controlled by fundamentalist supporters of Bass and Lee. They recommended their own slate of fundamentalist trustees. If approved, the same practice at the 2020 annual meeting would give fundamentalist control of the SBU board of trustees, enabling them to reverse previous trustee actions regarding the firing of Bass and reinstatement of Lee.

At the October 2019 state convention annual meeting, the fundamentalist domination was painfully evident. Incriminating and unfounded information was placed on car windshields in the parking lot. Those entering the convention center were given pamphlets attacking the SBU actions and supporting Bass and Lee. President Turner's annual report was attacked by only fundamentalist questions with no time allowed for defenders of SBU to speak. The nominating committee trustee recommendation was also supported by only anti-SBU attacks and no SBU supporters were allowed to speak.

Dr. Turner's evaluation was very accurate: "It was a case of retaliation instead of reconciliation." It was typical of the historic process of fundamentalist takeover practices for the past four decades.

Addressing a concerned SBU faculty and administration, Dr. Turner offered his evaluation of the situation:

"Make no mistake about it- the controversy in which SBU has been embroiled has little to do with theology; this has been a co-opted controversy used by others as an attempt to exert undue influence over the university. The manipulation, underhandedness, and self-dealing threatens who SBU has always been, and I cannot help but think the Lord is displeased."

Friends:

Besides the political division caused by the fundamentalists, the great personal effect on friends of mine hurt the most for me. Friends I had made on the national and state level denominations were forced to leave their key leadership positions. Although new denominations were formed for the ousted friends, the hurt was very evident. Churches were becoming divided over unnecessary loyalties required for membership and giving. Some of the best traditional college and seminary professors were forced to leave their positions to join in newly established graduate school programs or joined with other denominational programs.

These dismissals by new fundamentalist leadership were done in more inquisitorial fashion than in brotherly love and attempts of reconciliation. The actions were motivated by political power with a smokescreen of doctrinal purity. An editor for a local Springfield, Missouri, newspaper, accurately described the takeover actions not as a matter of conservative versus liberal, but more of the "tolerants versus the intolerants."

That is a rather lengthy accounting of my personal experiences with the radical fundamentalists. My relationships with other fundamentalists in churches, associations and denominations have been very cordial and respectful. Although there were disagreements over some theological positions, these were accepted with the greater understanding of Christian love and brotherhood.

Bob Perry
Denomination:

The environment in which I grew up in southwest Missouri was not without its biases and bigotry. Racism was very much a fact with the application of Jim Crow laws, and it was not at all rare to hear people use the "n" word with no shame or hesitation.

There was also a good amount of religious bigotry. Protestants were by far the largest and most dominant religious group, with Southern Baptists, in most towns, being the largest. In Verona, where I grew up, the second largest religious presence was Catholic with a sizable parish and a grades 1-6 elementary school. Entering the seventh grade most of the Catholic students came to the public high school.

My awareness of Catholics was that Baptists taught their children that Catholics were not really Christians. They worshipped statues, prayed to the Virgin Mary, and paid money to get deceased relatives out of purgatory. The worst thing a Baptist young person could do would be date a Catholic, or God forbid, marry a Catholic. I recall hearing Catholics referred to as "mackerel munchers," because they ate fish on Fridays.

Another group Southern Baptists held in suspicion was the Fundamental Baptists. These were the loose union of independent Baptist churches that were centered in Baptist Bible College in Springfield, MO. BBC was started in 1950 by Rev. W. E. Dowell, who also served as pastor of High Street Baptist Church.

The Independent Fundamental Baptists considered Southern Baptists liberal and heretical. Even though the two groups largely shared basic doctrines in common, fundamentalists tended to be hypercritical of Southern Baptists. One of the primary national critics was Dr. John R. Rice, who published a paper called, "The Sword of the Lord," from 1934 to 1980.

Churches:
As a boy active in a small Southern Baptist church, I was made aware early on of a fear we had verging on paranoia. The widespread rumor was that we should always be watchful for a sizable group of fundamentalists that might come and join our church. Gaining a voting majority, they would then proceed to vote the church out of the Southern Baptist Convention and deliver it into the clutches of the Independent Fundamentalist Baptist movement. We were encouraged to always be on the alert for these "church-stealing" Baptists.

These were the impressions I had as a boy. I never heard a single account of this nefarious thing actually happening, though I suppose it could have. It left me with an attitude of suspicion toward this "other kind" of Baptist and the expectation that they would not approve of my faith.

I really knew very few Fundamental Baptists until I went to college in Springfield in 1962. After completing my freshman year, I had a summer job at a large shoe warehouse. The majority of the summer employees at the warehouse were BBC students. On a personal level, I found them to be likable and devout Christians, but they often questioned me about how I could stand to be a Southern Baptist.

While we ate our brown bag lunches at noon, the conversation would often turn to all that was wrong with the Southern Baptist Convention. The BBC students understood it to be a religious hierarchy with total control over the churches. I never succeeded in convincing them that SBC churches were entirely autonomous and their cooperation in giving, use of literature, etc. was voluntary.

Toward the end of the summer, I had become so troubled by this constant criticism of my faith, that I made an appointment to visit with my pastor, Dr. Thomas Field, at First Baptist Church of Springfield. Dr. Field was no stranger to this harsh and hateful criticism of Southern Baptists. The Sunday morning television airwaves in the Ozarks were dominated by the 11:00 service of First Baptist on one local channel, and the 11:00 service of High Street Baptist on the other channel. Dr. Dowell regularly used his Sunday morning sermon to criticize Southern Baptists in general and Dr. Field and First Baptist in particular.

Dr. Field was a gentleman and a scholar. He was considered a consummate orator, and an elegant preacher. The only time I ever saw him really angry was during our conversation about my BBC workmates. At one point he rose from his desk, went to his bookshelves, and pulled out a copy of the recently adopted 1963 version of the "Baptist Faith and Message." This was a summary of the basic beliefs held by Southern Baptists.

He handed me the copy of the BFM and said, "This is what we believe! Take this to them, and tell them to stuff it in their ... ears!" (I think I almost heard Dr. Field say a bad word.) After that he would check in with me about how it was going at work occasionally, and I would later be licensed to the Gospel Ministry by First Baptist.

Education:

Southern Baptists were growing throughout the 1950s and 1960s at a rapid pace. They had four well-established seminaries, but during these years they opened two more – Golden Gate Baptist Theological Seminary in the San Francisco area, and Midwestern Baptist Theological Seminary in Kansas City, MO. These would become fully accredited, respected institutions.

Baptist Bible College in Springfield was not accredited by the North Central Association (the primary accreditation agency for Missouri) until 2001. My impression was that fundamentalist schools focused more on "indoctrination" than "education." The difference being that indoctrination may involve rigorous study, but it is designed to reinforce and defend what you already believe. Education is a process to allow students to explore difficult issues honestly, ask appropriate questions and arrive at beliefs that are personally owned and understood.

This was my experience at Midwestern Seminary in the 1960s. Professors were devoted to the scriptures and had studied faithfully to understand God's revelation to mankind. Most of them were brilliant scholars and widely published authors. I was blessed to sit under the teaching of names like Honeycutt, Morton, Ashcraft, McCarty, Coble, Howell, Wamble, and others.

By and large, Southern Baptists had developed a system of education for future religious leaders that prepared them to "rightly divide the Word of truth." We were taught Baptists had no creed but the Bible, and that the scriptures were reliable and effective in guiding us to Christ and Christ-likeness.

Me and Fundamentalists

Chapter Two: Growing Presence of Fundamentalists

Paul Bass

Although Christian fundamentalism has been around for several centuries, their aggressive move into political practice and power is actually comparatively recent. They have certainly been active in local, state and national political campaigns as defenders of biblical principles. Most notable was its presence in the historical Scopes "monkey trial" of 1925 in Dayton, Tennessee. In the 1930s, they organized to form lists of "fundamental" doctrines as test of orthodoxy. Although the lists varied, one central theme was the "inerrancy and infallibility" of the Bible.

The results of these efforts were frustrated by the major national denominations. Accordingly, fundamentalists separated and formed their own independent churches. They became defined as "narrowly creedal and separatist." Lacking effective control of any major denomination, fundamentalist radicals began campaigns against some major denominations. In Texas, J. Frank Norris of Fort Worth, waged an ugly campaign against "Baylor University, Texas Baptists and the entire SBC." Such were the initial actions of the limited number of fundamentalists trying to impact the SBC.

Denominations:

Wanting to be accurate in an examination of fundamentalist strategy for political takeover of a major denomination, let us consider descriptions of the actions in the Southern Baptist Convention(SBC). The procedures and actions that have occurred, can also be identified in other major denominations.

The growing division among Southern Baptists can be summed up by identifying two camps. One side are the traditionalists who desire to "work together to carry the gospel to the world." On the other side were those with a "tendency to be exclusive and to use narrow tests of orthodoxy." These standards would be used first in election of convention leadership.

Before the 1979 annual SBC convention, two Texans sponsored plans for the initial steps of the takeover. Judge Paul Pressler of Houston and Dr. Paige Patterson of Dallas announced their plans to elect a "conservative" SBC president and "restore the convention to its historical roots." The term "historical roots" was from their non-historical definition. The 1979 SBC met in June in Houston. They found an attractive and popular candidate for the presidency in Adrian Rogers, pastor of Bellevue Church in Memphis, Tennessee. There were six announced candidates for the position. Through careful strategic planning, Rogers was elected on the first ballot. Every year following, the convention has elected a "conservative" president agreeable to the radical fundamentalists. In the SBC, the president exercises great political power in the appointment of the Committee on Committees and organization board suggestions.

The takeover of the Southern Baptist Convention was an intentional plot designed by the team of Patterson and Pressler. They understood that the real power in the organizations of the SBC was with the trustees of the institutions. The trustee appointment was largely controlled by the president of the SBC. In 1979, with the election of fundamentalist Adrian Rogers, the plot began to take shape. In September of 1980, Pressler stated publicly "that they "need to go for the jugular- we need to go for the trustees."

It is interesting to notice that to date Pressler and Patterson over time have found themselves in discredited situations. Pressler has been accused in court of "unwanted sexual contact and advances by multiple men." He is awaiting trial. Patterson was fired as the president of Southwestern Baptist Theological Seminary in Fort Worth, Texas, over the mishandling of rape allegations on campus. SBC President J. D. Grear urged SBC churches not to host Patterson in their pulpits.

For the next ten years, the SBC in their annual convention elected fundamentalist presidents and often narrowly approved the recommended committees and boards. By 1989, the fundamentalists were successful in controlling the majority of SBC boards and organizations. Those trustees would make some dramatic changes in the traditional work of those organizations. The Sunday School Board and SBC seminaries were the first to feel the impacts of new orthodoxy agreements. Many of the conservative leadership spread the message that perceived liberals dominated the existing seminaries. Many changes in leadership occurred with frightening results for many of the traditional convention members. Another hit for the seminaries was the loss of academic accreditation for some of their programs. Education for the SBC was changed from academic freedom to more of their orthodox indoctrination. The Education Commission of the SBC was eliminated.

In 1987 a number of Baptists disappointed in the direction of the SBC formed the Alliance of Baptists. In 1990, moderate Baptists joined with the more progressive Baptists in Atlanta, Georgia, to form the Cooperative Baptist Fellowship (CBF). It was felt strongly by the moderates that the conservative Baptists "had departed from Baptist distinctives." Today there are about 1900 churches in the CBF. They have supported schools and seminaries more in keeping with traditional Baptist guidelines.

Another major step taken by the SBC was the creation of the 2000 Baptist Faith and Message. For thirty-seven years Southern Baptists operated very well with the 1963 Baptist Faith and Message. It was not a creed, but a general statement of inclusion among believers alongside of historical Baptist teachings. The 2000 Baptist Faith and Message became the tool of the fundamentalist SBC leadership for exclusivity and to use as a narrow test of orthodoxy. All denominational workers were to comply with the statement to continue to be employed by all organizations of the SBC. It became a restrictive creed instead of a cooperative statement of inclusion. There were significant differences between the 1963 and 2000 statements. Much stronger emphasis was given to pastoral authority. There was strong denunciation of women in ministerial leadership and strict adherence to biblical "inerrancy and infallibility." The new version also deleted the principle that "Jesus Christ is the criterion by which scripture should be interpreted." What they had been unable to do in the 1930s was now the rule of law. There was a resignation of career missionaries, pastoral leadership and church departures from the SBC following the adoption of this new so-called statement of faith.

The race was now on to take control of the SBC state conventions. A growing organization of power hungry and orthodoxy enforcers began to infiltrate and enlist leaders within state convention organizations. Using the familiar and effective tactics of the past, many state conventions became pawns under the SBC fundamentalist leadership. Allowing for easier control of the state conventions was the departure of traditional Baptists and some churches to the newly formed Baptist conventions, such as the Cooperative Baptist Fellowship.

Churches:

Many traditional churches and church members were dissatisfied with the new directions and requirements of the SBC actions. Sharing from my knowledge of my home Missouri Baptist Convention, many churches were faced with the decision to be in total compliance or leave the convention. A number of the Missouri churches were denied continued membership because of their dual alignment. Efforts were also made locally to disallow church members to even contribute financially to other than SBC causes.

Education:

As has already been described, schools became a target for the fundamentalist takeover. It was important to politically control the Baptist state sponsored undergraduate schools. To achieve that goal, it was necessary to control the board of trustees of the schools. Using the same techniques to achieve control of the state conventions new board members were nominated by the state convention leadership. Their trustee recommendations were initially at odds with the traditional recommended trustees offered by the institution. Over a period of several years, it was easy to gain ultimate control of the board of trustees. That control allowed the schools to impose more rigid oversight of the individual faculty and administration members of the school. In most cases stringent adherence to the new doctrinal "statements of faith" was required for continued employment. As usual, the actions were for political control under a smokescreen of doctrinal purity. Several schools rebelled against the threatened takeovers with lawsuits settled by civil courts.

As a result, some schools with long histories in the state became independent of the state convention if charters permitted. Alumni and Baptists from the newly created separators of the SBC became supporters and adherents of these new schools. Some schools created graduate programs in Christian education to answer the control of the radical fundamentalists on the traditional SBC seminaries. Attendance at the traditional seminaries and new graduate programs prompted the creation of undergraduate studies at the traditional seminaries and the closing of some new graduate programs.

Seminaries began to produce classes of graduates more concerned with pastoral authority, independent church operations and narrowing theological alignment. They also were more submissive to the dictates of state convention leadership and directions.

Bob Perry

As I completed seminary and began my ministry as a pastor in the 1960s, my awareness of and interaction with fundamentalists grew. There was some presence of fundamentalist influence within the Southern Baptist Convention, but the denomination was generally dominated by leaders who were more mainline or tolerant.

Denominations:
Fundamentalism was always strong in Southwest Missouri. Springfield was a major center for the Baptist Bible Fellowship, but it was also the world headquarters for the Assemblies of God. That group was similar to Baptists in most basic beliefs, but they were considered a part of the Pentecostal movement. They emphasized the spiritual gifts, particularly speaking in tongues. They were generally somewhat more conservative and fundamentalist than Southern Baptists.

In the late 1940s, there was a conservative split from Northern Baptists (later to be called American Baptists). This group became the Conservative Baptist Association of America. I had an uncle who was a pastor and missionary with this group. They felt that the Northern Baptist Convention had slid into liberalism or modernism, and that the Southern Baptist Convention was not far behind.

In addition to these more formal denominational movements that tended toward fundamentalism, there was the emergence of the "charismatic movement" within many denominations. This movement brought the belief in spiritual healings and speaking in tongues into churches all over the country. The movement became a strong and divisive influence within major denominations, including Southern Baptists, Methodists, Episcopalians, Catholics, and practically all denominations.

Some Southern Baptist pastors aligned themselves with the charismatic movement, others resisted it and attempted to minimize its influence in local churches. Nearly all pastors of mainline churches had to deal with the movement in one way or another.

Churches:

Fundamentalist Baptist churches were among the first to build what today would be called megachurches. First Baptist Church of Hammond, Indiana was one of these. The pastor there, Jack Hyles, became well known and widely read because of his "success" in building a large church. Another of these was the Akron Baptist Temple in Akron, Ohio, which regularly had over 4,000 in Sunday attendance.

A part of the "success" of these churches was huge bus ministries. Churches would buy large fleets of used school buses and utilize them to transport large numbers of previously unchurched people (mostly children) to their buildings on Sunday mornings. These ministries depended on masses of trained volunteers who maintained the busses, did the driving, and did regular Saturday visitation at the homes of prospective bus riders.

Many Southern Baptist pastors, including this author, utilized bus ministry strategies to build up local churches. Some used refreshments, prizes and "hard-sell" evangelism of children to increase the numbers of baptisms. Most Southern Baptist pastors minimized these tactics, but many did use bus ministry, especially in the 1960s and 1970s.

Another phenomenon that was taking place during this time was a host of fundamentalist Baptist evangelists who were leading church members to doubt the validity of their "salvation" and redo their profession of faith in Christ and be "rebaptized." This also served to inflate the statistical success of churches.

Education:
In the late 1970s, the presence of judgmental fundamentalism moved from outside the Southern Baptist Convention to within the denomination. The Pressler-Patterson movement got under way, and in a relatively small number of years gained control of the denomination.

One of their primary targets for criticism was the "liberal professors" at the SBC seminaries. As a result, over time, all six SBC seminaries were brought under the control of the new Fundamentalist leadership. Seminary presidents were fired or forced out, professors were fired or forced out, and the whole atmosphere of theological education changed. Honest academic inquiry became less valued, and "doctrinal purity" came to be demanded.

When I decided to attend Midwestern Baptist Theological Seminary in 1967, I got a call from my uncle who was a Conservative Baptist missionary in Honduras scolding me for going to that "liberal" school and urging me to change my mind.

My Dad was the oldest of five brothers raised by a widowed, single mother. This uncle was the brother just younger than Dad. He had gone into the army and was shipped to Europe in World War II at the same time Dad was. But my uncle saw much more fighting than Dad. He was considered a war hero by the family, and he was much admired as a lifelong missionary in Latin America.

It was a great disappointment to me that I never had the approval or affirmation of this highly revered member of the family. My choices for theological education, denominational involvement and style of ministry never suited him. I was always grateful that my dad respected my convictions and stands even though he may not have been in full agreement with all of them.

I will always be grateful for the education I received at Midwestern Seminary in the 1960s (Master of Divinity) and 1970s (Doctor of Ministry).

Me and Fundamentalists

Chapter Three: Dominant Presence of Fundamentalists

Paul Bass

Denomination:

As more and more of the traditional Southern Baptists move into the newer Baptist denominations, the Southern Baptist Convention becomes stronger with total fundamentalist control of its national organization and boards. The SBC seminaries are declining in regular enrollments but are trying to keep financial pace by instituting undergraduate degree programs. Publication of church study materials has become more indoctrinating than educating. Missions programs- national and international- are also becoming more intolerant of differing, personal doctrinal views. Fortunately, those called into missions, but rejected by fundamentalist-controlled boards, can find other places of service in more tolerant, newer denominations.

States affiliated with the SBC are also becoming stronger and gaining more control of their institutions and organizations. Sadly, extended litigation by some states conventions over political control of those institutions and organizations has placed a burden on state and some church budgets. Decreased budgets will lead to a decrease in state ministry-oriented institutions. Among these are the state convention sponsored Baptist schools. The fundamentalist dominated boards of trustees will continue to force out popular accredited faculty and staff. There will be a challenge to maintain official accreditation. That will produce a lack of interest by serious students and their families.

Churches:
Churches are being challenged to financially support the state convention institutions and organizations, but also ongoing legal actions within their state. This is resulting in some churches having to adjust their budget operations. Some church members who dare to contribute outside of the church-approved budget are not able to contribute to outside Baptist causes. Serious threats of loss of membership have been given to those who dare to contribute to these outside causes.

As more fundamentalist leadership is taking control of these churches, decision making responsibilities are being absorbed by the pastor and elders. The average church member is expected only to attend and give- not to assume any operating authority. Responsibilities of the average church members participating in committees and/or boards is becoming a practice of the past.

In many of these churches, worship has become entertainment. The use of repetitive praise choruses is replacing the singing of traditional hymns. Biblical preaching has become more "indoctrinational" instead of serious expository including consideration of differing views.

Education:
Total control of Southwest Baptist University (and other affiliated MBC institutions) by the fundamentalist controlled Missouri Baptist Convention was achieved in the October 2020. This domination was achieved through several actions preceding the October 2020 annual state convention.

To strengthen their control over SBU, the MBC Executive Board met on August 25, 2020 and announced new procedures for the approval of affiliated institutions new board of trustee members. The long-standing, cooperative system of the institutions recommending new trustees for the MBC Nominating Committee submission was discarded.

Institutions would no longer have any role in recommending new trustees. It was now totally under the action of the MBC Nominating Committee. In addition, when the committee report would be presented at the annual meeting, there would be no opposition allowed to be expressed.

MBC leadership met with the SBU Board of Trustees in September and announced the addition of an additional layer of "basic fundamental doctrines" required for all instructors in the Redford School of Theology. The three new creedal statements required for affirmation are

infallible, biblical inerrancy; the subservient role of women; and other issues of human sexuality. All professors must affirm their acceptance of these additional doctrinal layers after the MBC officially approves these in their annual meeting.

With the anticipated new trustees appointed at the October 2020 annual convention, the SBU Board of Trustees will be totally dominated by the fundamentalist controlled MBC leadership. With the new procedures imposed on the Redford School of Theology, there will likely be a mass exodus of faculty members and students.

The MBC fundamentalists' ultimate goal had been achieved over a period of several painful years. The lives of faculty and students were disregarded in favor of political power and the smokescreen of "doctrinal purity."

It is harder to enlist young people from these churches to attend their local Baptist colleges. Fewer of these students are considering a call to the full time ministry. Of the students acknowledging a call to the ministry, most are pursuing starting independent churches or bivocational social ministries.

The idea of a God-called, well-educated minister may be a thing of the past. With colleges and seminaries offering Baptist indoctrination instead of academic study, the well-trained, openminded minister is now a rarity in SBC churches and schools.

Bob Perry

In 1981, I attended the first annual meeting of the Southern Baptist Convention that I had been able to attend in several years. From 1973 to 1980, my family and I served as missionaries in Latin America through the Southern Baptist Foreign Mission Board. We returned to the U. S. in May of 1980, and I became the pastor of a mid-sized First Baptist Church in the Kansas City, MO area. The 1981 meeting in Los Angeles was my first opportunity to attend the SBC after getting settled back in the states.

We had found it necessary to resign from our missionary work due to health issues with the family. My wife, Nancy, and I had both had hepatitis, typhoid, and salmonella while living in Mexico. Our oldest son, Doug, was 13 when we came home, and our younger son, David, was 9. David had been suffering for several months from painful and severe respiratory problems from breathing the polluted air of Mexico City. The smog was almost a constant problem in the city, with some experts saying it was the equivalent of smoking two packs of cigarettes a day. Our doctor advised us to get David out of that environment. In January of 1980, we sent him to live with his grandparents in Southwest Missouri. Finally, to reunite the family, we decided to leave the field in May of that year.

When I entered the convention hall where the SBC was being held, I immediately sensed that something was different from any previous convention I had attended. First, I noticed that there was an exceptionally large crowd for an SBC meeting on the west coast. This area was not a stronghold for Southern Baptists, and it was a long trip for most to attend. Second, the entire atmosphere was different. There was tension in the air, and the usual feeling of a big family reunion was not there. No more a family reunion; it was now a political rally where people like me who were not aligned with the political movement under way were not welcome. Third, the sermons that were preached at the Pastors Conference prior to the convention were more strident and judgmental than I had experienced before. It felt like a fire-and-brimstone style of preaching, with an angry crowd not just saying the occasional "Amen" to a preacher's point, but shouting and applauding tag lines that essentially created an "us" and "them" atmosphere.

Finally, once business sessions began, there was an obvious effort to control the agenda. The microphones on the floor where individual messengers could speak were turned on and off by sound technicians who followed the instructions of the chair as to who could be heard. There were long lines at microphones, indicating that some had been notified in advance of what issue was coming up and what should be said about it.

I was deeply disturbed by the whole "feel" of the convention, when some friends called to my attention that many people being nominated and elected to leadership at the convention were not strong supporters of the Cooperative Program. I had just spent seven years on the mission field with my family being supported by the Cooperative Program (CP). This was Southern Baptists' unified financial program for supporting the work of the denomination, especially the mission work done by the Foreign Mission Board and the Home Mission Board. It had long been a norm that those elected to leadership in the denomination demonstrated loyalty to the work by leading their churches to give generously to the CP. Many churches gave 10% or more of their annual receipts to support the work of missions.

In a later business session, I saw Dr. Kenneth Chafin get the floor to call attention to this new phenomenon and offer an alternative candidate to replace a nominee whose church gave less than 1% annually to the CP. I do not recall whether his effort was successful or not, but I made a beeline for Dr. Chafin as soon as he walked away from the microphone. I introduced myself to him, expressed my appreciation for his effort, and asked what I could do to help stem this disturbing trend in the SBC. He warmly greeted me and told me about a group that had begun meeting to try to inform Southern Baptists about what was an organized movement to take political control and "purge" the denomination of "liberals." He indicated that the group did not yet have any Missouri representative, and he invited me to the next meeting of the group.

My initial involvement in the resistance to the fundamentalists was based on missions. I did not want to see the heart for missions cut out of the convention by electing leaders who did not wholeheartedly support the work. I felt that the hypocrisy of encouraging rank-and-file Southern Baptists to continue to give generously to missions, while their elected leaders set poor examples of giving would eventually do great damage to the work. Soon I would learn of the theological agenda that was part of the political control effort and how that would exclude and ostracize thousands of faithful and free Baptists.

That began my involvement in what had come to be known as "The Gatlinburg Gang." One of the early meetings of the group was convened in Gatlinburg, Tennessee, thus the name. The first meeting I attended was held at a camp near Knoxville, Tennessee. There I met men whom I came to see as giants of wisdom and integrity. The leaders were Cecil Sherman and Ken Chafin. Sherman was pastor of First Baptist Church of Asheville, North Carolina. Chafin had been a professor of evangelism at Southern Baptist Theological Seminary and the dean of the Billy Graham Schools of Evangelism that were held prior to Billy Graham Crusades. In 1972, Chafin had been called as pastor of South Main Baptist Church in Houston, Texas. These two men were prescient in seeing the pain and destruction that was ahead for Southern Baptists as fundamentalists took control of all the levers of power. The "purge" was on its way.

Others in the group when I came on board were Bill Bruster, pastor in the Knoxville area, Vernon Davis, pastor of First Baptist of Alexandria, Virginia, Bill Sherman (Cecil's younger brother and pastor in Nashville, TN), Jim Slatton from Virginia, Lavonn Brown from Oklahoma, and number of others. I will not attempt to mention all of these heroes because a number of volumes have been written to record this history more accurately and in greater detail than I could. One such book is *The Struggle for the Soul the SBC*, edited by Dr. Buddy Shurden.

This was the beginning of the fundamentalist takeover of the Southern Baptist Convention. What started in 1979 was pretty well completed by 1986. Fundamentalism that had been a nuisance of legalistic and judgmental criticism of the SBC from the outside, became a juggernaut working on the inside to change the SBC forever. As the movement grew within the SBC, it quickly spread to the state conventions across the country. Even state conventions that initially expressed opposition, or at least disdain, for the politicization of Baptist life, eventually fell under the pressure.

Out of the controversy there were good things that came into being. As an alternative to the very politicized Pastors Conference held just prior to the Convention each year, "moderate" Baptists began The Southern Baptist Forum as an alternative event. Eventually The Forum gave birth to the Cooperative Baptist Fellowship (CBF), which became an alternative mission support channel and later a denomination-like structure for moderates. The Alliance of Baptists formed in the early years of the conflict. Many new seminaries were founded in Texas, Virginia, Kentucky and elsewhere. New attention and support were directed by CBF toward Central Seminary, an American Baptist school in the Kansas City area.

The constant infighting that characterizes fundamentalism has continued in the Southern Baptist Convention. Once most of the moderates were cleansed from the SBC agencies and institutions, other "enemies of the faith" were found. The architects of the takeover,

Paige Patterson and Paul Pressler, were eventually discredited, but the fires of criticism and inquisition they lit continued to burn. Calvinism became a dividing line between Southern Baptists, as that theological position grew in popularity among younger pastors. Pastors who had not been aligned with the original group that executed the takeover were often regarded with suspicion no matter how conservative they were. Any pastor or teacher who endorsed women in ministry was considered unacceptable.

The SBC came to be more and more aligned with the political right wing in the country, and formed close alliances with the Republican Party. The denomination that had once championed the separation of church and state was now promoting prayer in public schools, vouchers for the support of private schools, and frequent invitations of Republican candidates to speak at church and denominational meetings. Candidates were implicitly, if not openly, endorsed by leading Southern Baptist pastors.

For many of us who were nurtured and blessed by our Southern Baptist heritage, it has been sad to see what has happened to the SBC. The very system that taught us about the "priesthood of the believer," the "autonomy of the local church," the freedom of interpretation of scripture under the guidance of the Holy Spirit, and Jesus Christ as the ultimate revelation of God by which we understand the written Word, had now retreated from these principles.

The SBC was "sold a bill of goods." The people were told by the Patterson-Pressler crowd that there would be a new revival of evangelism and missions if they forced the "liberals" out of Southern Baptist life. That has not happened. They were told the seminaries would grow and prosper if the bad professors were fired and the right professors were brought in. That growth and flourishing has not happened. The people were told that there would be peace and harmony in the SBC once the "heretics" were purged. That certainly has not happened.

That has left exiles from the SBC like Paul Bass and myself to look for "islands of health and harmony" in a sea of denominational chaos and craziness. We find those islands of sanity here and there in a healthy local church, in a small upstart denomination-like structure, or in some of the more inclusive and progressive groups that have survived, like the Baptist World Alliance and the Baptist Joint Committee. We have claimed the freedom to carefully consider the channels for mission and ministry that honor traditional Baptist values and express what we understand to be the calling of God on our lives. For that freedom, we are grateful and joyful.

Me and Fundamentalists

Chapter Four: Practices of Fundamentalists

Paul Bass and Bob Perry

As we have experienced the actions of fundamentalists for over twenty-five years, we have discovered certain patterns and tactics used by the fundamentalists to gain control of a major denomination, its institutions and many of its churches. Many of these actions are far beneath the standards of Christian teachings and expected Christian behavior.

First, is the hidden agenda in their stated goals. Their true purpose is political control using a smokescreen of theological correctness. The idea is that God is only on their side of any theological question. Justified by end result, deceitfulness and even lying are acceptable practices. The purpose of their control of educational institutions is to practice indoctrination instead of education and academic freedom.

Second, their purposes and goals are usually discussed by a small, invited group of like-minded believers that meet in secret. Opposing viewpoints are not represented or welcome. While claiming to be empowered as God's secret service, they are acting very contrary to any scriptural teaching regarding disputes or disagreements within the broader fellowship.

Third, they are committed to spreading their criticisms and tactics in falsified public propaganda campaigns. These campaigns include carefully scripted personal attacks with half truths or outright lies. There is little opportunity for those in opposition to respond to the attacks. There is usually no personal, direct confrontation between the accuser and the accused.

Fourth, when there is the rare opportunity for public discussion (especially in official business sessions), use of prejudicial and very biased witnesses are employed and limited (if any) opposition points of view are allowed.

Fifth, there is the need to create an enemy. This created enemy serves to justify their superior positions and distracts from their tactics and main purposes. The creation of the enemy usually involves indirect reports from spies, misinterpretations of printed documents or outright lies.

Sixth, and very important, is the lack of scriptural procedure in dealing with disagreement in the fellowship of believers. For the fundamentalists, it more a matter of "retaliation instead of reconciliation." The results lead to exclusivity instead of inclusivity of membership.

Seventh, for a small, determined group to assume control of an organization, they must find where the polity, processes or traditions of the group have flaws and exploit those. In the case of the Southern Baptist Convention, that vulnerability was the bylaws that established that the annually elected president of the convention could single-handedly appoint the powerful Committee on Boards, which in turn made all of the nominations for trustees for all SBC agencies. Patterson and Pressler saw that if they could elect their person as president and control his appointments for a period of years in a row, all agencies could be stacked with trustees who would carry out their wishes.

Denomination:

The above listed practices have allowed fundamentalist leadership to maneuver control of convention programs and operations. The clandestine activities have permitted the majority of SBC membership unable to attend the conventions to have any voice in convention decisions.

It is interesting that the takeover of the SBC occurred at the same time as the national political situation saw the creation of the "moral majority." Some of the same players were involved in both events. It is regrettable that the message of fundamentalists and the moral majority became more political than scriptural.

Convention leadership led in a campaign to eliminate any church not in total compliance with new convention policies. State conventions and associations followed in that campaign on a local level.

Churches:
The impact on many local churches created division and concern for budget priorities. Church leadership funneled to pastor/elder control of business agendas and decisions. Church membership responsibilities lessened from committees and boards to observer status. Dissent and opposition to pastoral/elder leadership was not tolerated.

Conscious efforts by pastor/elder leadership attempted to rid the church of any members not in total support of the direction and decisions made.

Education:
If the fundamentalists claim to be more scripturally and doctrinally sound, they have a challenge to explain the clear biblical teachings in Matthew 18 and I Corinthians 6 in dealing with their brothers in Christ. A review of the passages is necessary.

Matthew18:15-17: If one of my followers sins against you, go and point out what was wrong. But do it in private, just between the two of you. If that person listens, you have won back a follower. But if that one refuses to listen, take along one or two others. The Scriptures teach that every complaint must be proven by two or more witnesses. If the follower refuses to listen to them, report the matter to the church. Anyone who refuses to listen to the church must be treated like an unbeliever or a tax collector. (Contemporary English Version)

I Corinthians6:1-8: When one of you has a complaint against another, do you take your complaint to a court of sinners? Or do you take it to God's people? Don't you know that God's people will judge the world? And if you are going to judge the world, can't you settle small problems? Don't you know we will judge the angels? And if this is so, we can surely judge everyday matters. Why do you take everyday complaints to judges who are not respected by the church? I say this to your shame. Aren't any of you wise enough to act as a judge between one follower and another? Why should one of you take another to be tried by unbelievers?

When one of you takes another to court, all of you lose. It would be better to let yourselves be cheated and robbed. But instead, you cheat and rob other followers. (Contemporary English Version)

In the past, fundamentalist leaders have explained that the I Corinthians passage deals with individual Christians, not Christian corporations. That distinction may be convenient, but it is not an accurate interpretation.

There is concern that the education of pastors at the seminary level has devolved from serious scriptural and academic preparation to a program of indoctrination to the new style of pastor/elder domination of church polity.

Summary of the Practices:

Here is your recipe for gaining control of a church-related organization. This is not a secret recipe like the Colonel's fried chicken; it is fairly obvious and widely known. But it works if one has the determination and discipline (and lacks ethics) to carry it out.

1. Have a clear but unspoken goal to gain political control, but hide it behind a high-sounding and righteous aim of spirituality and renewing or purifying the organization.

2. Create a small, secretive group of like-minded persons to devise and execute an intricate plan to systematically gain control. Make membership in this group a source of pride with the tacit promise of great rewards for those who remain faithful to the cause.

3. Set up a communication mechanism to spread criticism and accusations toward existing leadership. This may be done by mail, email, telephone, social media, printed materials or any other available means. Break down the trust that people have in their current leaders.

4. Control the platform and squelch open discussion at any opportunity where rank-and-file members might be able to express themselves or get truthful and unbiased information.

5. Create a "straw man" and attack him viciously. The straw man is an imaginary figure that does not exist in reality. He is clothed with an exaggerated garment of guilt based on half truths, out-of-context statements or outright lies. The straw man may be loosely based on a "liberal professor" or "heretical leader."

6. Ignore all scriptural principles and teachings that would encourage direct and open conversation or efforts at reconciliation.

7. Find the vulnerabilities in the organization and how it operates. Exploit those flaws to allow the determined and vocal minority to assume control.

Combine all of these ingredients, stir in some anger and hatred, proclaim divine leadership, and your goal of control will have been achieved.

Me and Fundamentalists

Chapter Five: Dangers of Fundamentalists

Paul Bass and Bob Perry

Let us emphasize that we are talking about the dangers of radical fundamentalists. Rational fundamentalism is a necessary force to balance our desire for inclusion of all believers. When one extreme, fundamentalist or liberal, dominates any religious organization, it results in exclusivism and divisiveness.

Denomination:
Baptists are not unique in denominational squabbles in the past fifty years. Most other mainstream denominations have had controversies over political, worship and doctrinal matters. It is usually developed over tradition versus practices affected by changing social standards. Finances are also an important factor in some of these divisions.

These divisions have allowed for the creation of more independent groups not aligned with any particular denomination. There is also the growth of subgroups within major denominations usually supportive of more fundamental or liberal positions on key issues. These subgroups have often drawn key leadership away from the mainstream denominations.

Of more long-term significance has been a decline of membership participation and identification. A balanced program of denominational history has been forgotten or overlooked. Across the board, denominations have seen a dramatic decrease in the number of students interested in pursuing a career in denominational ministry.

The fundamentalists extremists have created much of this division and turmoil. They claim to have an inside track with God regarding Christian leadership and doctrinal purity. They provide little room for disagreement and have been successful in demanding total obedience to their particular beliefs and practices. This has had an impact on the denominations' educational and outreach programs.

Churches:
Perhaps on the local level, the impact of denominational division has had its greatest impact. In many cases, the division not only hurts church unity, but creates divisions within the families of the church. Differences of opinion become very personal and the art of compromise and reconciliation suffers. Judgmental actions and opinions become more important than Christian love, acceptance or just forbearance.

Traditional activities in ministry and worship are affected. Changes are hard even when those charges occur with majority approval of the church membership. The church's outreach attitude and practices are also affected. Sometimes churches become more obsessed with who they get out instead of who they get in.

Because of these divisions, church finances also suffer. Church programs and ministries often suffer along with cutbacks in staff and denominational program support. Communities become very aware of church difficulties and have less positive consideration of the church's local role. Membership in many of the affected churches has accelerated the trend toward decline. In fact, some of these churches ignore the significance of an official church membership. They gear more toward numbers. Less emphasis on church membership and playing for entertainment in worship allows the leadership more dictatorial control of church business decisions. This creates a church attender with no meaningful church responsibilities.

Education:
As has been mentioned, denominational control by fundamental extremists has created major changes in denominational education. In particular, seminaries have moved more toward denominational indoctrination and away from true academic integrity. Denominations and the

church leadership they produce only support the less democratic and more dictatorial role of church staff and leadership. The decrease in seminary attendance has also challenged the traditional undergraduate denominational schools. Seminaries have resorted to establishing their own undergraduate programs to promote attendance and financial stability.

The fundamentalists extremists' control over denominational undergraduate institutions has created an atmosphere of theological indoctrination instead of academic freedom. Talented staff and faculty have left these schools to find places of more tolerance and academic orientation. Many schools attempting to maintain strong academic stability in the face of the challenge of young people being called to the ministry have been forced to close their doors.

Summary of the Dangers:

With apologies to Theodore Roosevelt, today's fundamentalists have become "bullies of the pulpit." They have taken personal control of many of our traditional and newer Baptist churches. They have taken personal control of the Southern Baptist Convention and its institutions. They have taken direct control of many of our longstanding Baptist colleges and universities. They have been directly responsible for the crises in the lives of many "fellow believers" in the field of education.

Our traditional practices of denominational unity, democratic participation of each church member and academic freedom in our educational institutions are becoming only memories of a past era. The authoritarian position of the pastor is sadly the new normal for many churches. The new board of elders has replaced the responsibility of regular church members who feel called to serve on church boards and committees. Regular church business meetings have become rubber stamps for predetermined actions and policies of the pastor/elders.

The role of the regular church member in these churches has become one of a worship spectator and financial supporter. Worship services in these churches have become more "pep rallies" than contemplative personal encounters with God. The church staffs have adopted more of a role as cheerleaders instead of personal ministers.

Me and Fundamentalists

Chapter Six: Future of Fundamentalists

Paul Bass and Bob Perry

These thoughts are based on the authors' expectations from past observations and experiences.

Denomination:
It is unlikely that the Southern Baptist Convention will ever return to the inclusive, education-minded organization that it was half a century ago. It is unlikely that the Southern Baptist Convention will ever reach out to the split off groups for reunification.

It is likely that it will continue to self-perpetuate its radical fundamentalist leadership in its organization, institutions and boards. It will attract some new fundamentalist-leaning groups willing to submit to leadership dictates.

The leadership has imposed strict interpretation and application of so-called statements of faith on its institutions and affiliated churches. It is likely that it will continue to add additional interpretation and application to its organization in an effort to alienate any attempted challenge to its leadership. In some ways it is likely that the fundamentalists will compete to "out-fundamentalize" each other for so-called scriptural authority and political control.

Resulting leadership competition may lead to further division and formation of new splinter groups. The core organization of Southern Baptists will likely stay financially sound (with the exception of extended lawsuits over defiant institutional control). The international and national mission efforts will probably continue to decline. More aggressive local and state recruitment will continue. Leadership will continue to be politically active nationally as long as their voices will be recognized and respected.

Business sessions in denominational meetings will be well-planned in advance with voting results predetermined. Any opposition to leadership plans will not be tolerated with only supportive speakers allowed.

Churches:
Churches within the fundamentalist-dominated denomination will continue until their limit of tolerance for oversight is reached. Churches will then drop out or move toward independent-minded operations. New pastors from the fundamentalist-dominated educational institutions will create or lead churches into the pastor/elder dictatorial operations. Church membership will be based on attendance and cooperation. Representation of churches at denominational meetings will be more pastor/elder dominated. Business meetings in the church will be on a limited basis with only business items brought that have been approved by the pastor/elder leadership. Any opposition to the leadership plans will be very limited if tolerated at all. Educational programs will be carefully controlled with only fundamentalist teaching accepted.

Education:
As the fundamentalists take over educational institutions, the demands for submission and adherence to dictated allegiances will increase over time. Lack of adequate administration over academic requirements for accreditation will have an impact on recruitment of faculty and students. A lack of adequate acceptable supervision of hiring and firing of faculty and staff will follow.

An example of this was seen in the Missouri Baptist Convention forcing of their five nominees for trustees to Southwest Baptist University in October 2019. One of the trustees had not been properly vetted for his past handling of a child sexual abuse case by his church staff member. An investigation by the entire board of trustees resulted in attacks by the MBC leadership against SBU.

Instead of being concerned about the main issue of the Missouri Baptist recommended trustee's hidden past failure, the Missouri Baptist leaders chose to accuse Southwest Baptist of an unfounded attack on their elected trustee. Instead of using the occasion to objectively investigate the incident, Missouri Baptists used the occasion to further attack Southwest Baptist University. Such will be the continued vindictive future of fundamentalists in "cooperating" with their brothers in Christ.

Summary of the Future:

Those maintaining and expanding political control of Southern Baptist Convention agencies and institutions have too often employed the practice of "the end justifies the means." Sadly, many of of those practices have been less than Christlike.

The past memories of a unified Southern Baptist Convention meeting for annual meetings to worship, fellowship and conduct open business is gone. The idea of all Baptists joining together for missions, education and evangelism with a common purpose and under a unified budget is gone. Hopefully, these traditional memories and practices can be somewhat restored within the newer, Baptist organizations.

A wise counselor said that "we have not left the Southern Baptist Convention; the Southern Baptist Convention has left us!"

Me and Fundamentalists

Conclusion
Paul Bass and Bob Perry

Dr. J. D. Grey was the former pastor of the First Baptist Church, New Orleans, Louisiana, and former president of the Southern Baptist Convention. He had the feeling that the early actions of fundamentalists in their takeover attempt was a political pendulum swing in the convention and the convention would adjust over time and swing back to more moderate control. He died sadly with the disappointment that his view was wrong and that the fundamentalists only grew in their domination and control.

The presence of fundamentalist control is not likely to be altered. It is also not likely to ever change into a more inclusive fellowship reaching out to brother and sister Baptists in the newer fellowships. Their unscrupulous practices continue today in a continuation of state and institutional political control.

How are we as believers to deal with fundamentalism? Sadly, we must tolerate its presence. We also have a responsibility to educate and warn other believers of their goals and tactics. (Thus the purpose for this book!)

For a group of people claiming scriptural authority, practice and primacy, the actions used are very contradictory. First, Jesus' commands in the New Testament that when a brother is accused of errant teachings or actions, he is to be personally confronted. If the errors continue, the accuser is to again meet with him and witnesses. If the error persists, then he is to be dismissed from fellowship and association. That practice has rarely, if ever, been followed.

Second, when there is a controversy in the fellowship, both sides are to be fairly represented for prayerful consideration. Again, that practice has rarely, if ever, been followed.

Third, the fellowship is to make conscious efforts to restore an errant brother back into the fellowship. Again, that practice has rarely, if ever, been followed.

A religious editor for the *Springfield News-Leader* observed wisely early on that the division in the SBC was less about fundamentalist versus moderates, but more correctly as "tolerants versus intolerants." A wise, Arkansas, country pastor told me years ago that "when a church spends more time trying to get people out than get people in, it is in real trouble." That holds true on a national convention, state convention and associational level.

It is also very important for people to carefully screen the barrage of propaganda we are faced with each day through all forms of media- even from some pulpits. A wise college professor of mine said, "Even an old cow spits out the cockle burrs before she swallows the hay."

We would remind our fundamentalist fellow believers of the wisdom in Proverbs 11:29: "He who troubles his own house will inherit the wind." The Contemporary English Version translation is even more plain: "Fools who cause trouble in the family won't inherit a thing." We all need to remember that those things we do in God's name on earth have eternal consequences for us and others.

We, who are part of God's Kingdom on the earth, should try to learn to live with those with whom we will share the Kingdom of heaven. While some fundamentalists may question our salvation and whether we will make it to heaven, we do not question the legitimacy of their faith in Christ. So, we expect to spend eternity with many fundamentalists. With that being the case, we try to love them and pray for them as we live in this "waiting room" for heaven.

It was Edwin Markham who said, "He drew a circle that shut me out- Heretic, rebel, a thing to flout. But love and I had the wit to win: We drew a circle and took him in!" Jesus' commands are clear.

A marriage therapist was telling a man he should forgive and love his estranged ex-wife. The man said, "she is no longer my wife, so I don't have to love her." The therapist reminded him that Jesus also told us to love our neighbors. He responded, "she doesn't live anywhere near my neighborhood anymore." So, the therapist reminded the man that Jesus also told us to love our enemies. He replied, "Okay, that one got me."

Although some rather harsh, personal and accusatory charges have been made against the fundamentalists, even in this book, we are constantly reminded of our obligation as believers to adhere to Paul's teachings in I Corinthians 13 to love one another. The model of Jesus to "love the sinner and hate the sin" also has applications for brothers in Christ. It is very important to remember that we all will answer to God in eternity for our actions here on earth. May God grant us all the ability to be followers of Jesus' example in our thoughts and actions.

Me and Fundamentalists

Addendum: Fundamentalists in the Scriptures and History

Paul Bass and Bob Perry

Can a case be made for the presence of fundamentalists in the Bible? Is the rise of fundamentalism a modern product or has it been existent throughout history? The answer largely depends on the definition of "fundamentalism."

If you define fundamentalism as "individuals who fought for political control while using the smokescreen of scriptural inerrancy and doctrinal purity," then you can find examples in the Scriptures, the early church and throughout church history. In the Middle Ages, some church leadership used new doctrinal teachings and interpretations for financial gain and continued political leadership. Other church leaders used questions of doctrinal purity to eliminate rivals and threatened rebellions.

Were there actually radicals who fought for political control while using the smokescreen of scriptural inerrancy and doctrinal purity in the Bible itself?

Old Testament:

There are a few examples in the Old Testament of such people who tried to achieve political control of God's people while claiming special teachings from God.

(I Kings 13:11-25) An example of the conflict between two prophets of God is found in this scripture. A younger prophet from Judah had performed a miracle for King Jeroboam. An older prophet heard about the miracle and invited the younger prophet into his house. The younger prophet had been forbidden by God to eat bread and drink water. The older prophet lied to the younger prophet and assured him that God had told him it was okay to eat bread and drink water. The younger prophet ate bread and drank water. The older prophet finally confessed his lie to the younger prophet. God told the younger prophet that since he obeyed the older prophet instead of obeying Him, he would lose his life. After he left the older prophet's house, he was attacked by a lion and died, with his body left by the roadside for others to view. (Contemporary English Version)

The warning was that there were consequences for any man who disobeyed God's calling. In spite of the younger prophet's earlier great miracle, he still disobeyed God and suffered the consequences. Part of the fundamentalist practice is to assume priority over God's previous calling and teachings. There are indeed consequences for all who accept the authority of any other person than God himself.

(I Kings 22:7-35) Another example of interest is Zedekiah. He was the leader of 400 prophets in the Northern Kingdom serving under the evil King Ahab. Zedekiah was a political hack supporting every military decision made by King Ahab with words of assurance from God.

When Ahab joined forces with the Southern Kingdom to fight a battle, he sought confirmation from Zedekiah and the 400 prophets. A lone prophet, Micaiah, dared to disagree and forecast a defeat. Zedekiah was irate that Micaiah would dare to challenge his authority to speak for God. Zedekiah slapped Micaiah in public and Micaiah was sent to prison for defiance. Micaiah's words of prophecy came true with a major defeat. There is no other mention of either prophet.

Zedekiah saw himself as the only and true word from God. No other exceptions were to be allowed. He was more committed to King Ahab than to the God he claimed to represent. This serves as a dangerous warning about fundamentalists who seek political approval and favor rather than obedience to God.

(Esther) The character of Haman in the book of Esther is a prime example of a person using the legal requirement for worship of the king to persecute others and seek his own political gain. When Esther, a Jew, became queen, Haman conspired with others to initiate a legal requirement for all in the kingdom to worship the king. He knew that the Jews would not submit to such a practice and would face the death penalty. His prejudice and desire for political gain in the kingdom was sought using the smokescreen of religious purity. Only God's intervention through Esther would defeat his purpose and bring about Haman's own death.

New Testament:
In the New Testament, examples of such attempted leadership are more prevalent. Jesus faced such experiences in his day and as recorded in the Gospels.

Pharisees- Their voice was the only authoritative word from God. They would not accept any other spiritual insights. They had to have total control of their religious organization. They had to create enemies to attack.

Gnostics- They alone had unique spiritual insight. They would impart their spiritual wisdom for a price. They were disruptive to early churches. They viciously attacked any opponents.

Church History:
The early church faced its share of political power grabbers who used the smokescreen of scriptural inerrancy and doctrinal purity as excuses for control. Examples from centuries past might include:

Roman Catholic hierarchy-
They held significant complete political and religious power locally and universally. They did not tolerate opposing viewpoints and practices. They were inhumane in their treatment and intolerance of dissenters. They felt justified in publicly burning "heretics" at the stake.

Inquisition-
They demanded obedience and submission to religious authorities. They demanded acceptance of all church edicts and doctrines. They became extremists in using physical torture to compel confession and submission.

Protestant Intolerance-
They fought the attacks of heresy from the Catholics. They became intolerant of the different views within the fellowships. They dealt punishment and banishment for dissenters within and also sponsored torture and executions. (Anabaptists, etc.)

Even the Puritans, having established in the new world for religious freedom, would deny the same religious freedom to those who disagreed with them.

In Ken Follet's 2017 best seller book, *A Column of Fire*, the battle between Catholics and Protestants in the 1500s is chronicled. One of the main characters explained her evaluation of the public and private battles:

"But Margery at forty-five no longer believed that Protestantism was evil and Catholicism perfect. For her the important divide was between tyranny and tolerance; between people who tried to force their views on everyone else, and the people who respected the faith of those who disagreed with them."

The concept of fundamentalists desiring political control in religious organizations is not a recent practice. Examples throughout history give evidence of their presence. It is also a clear warning of their continued presence in the future.

Afterword

Following completion of the final book draft, anticipated results of the fundamentalists' domination of Southwest Baptist University happened sooner than expected.

First, on October 20, the *Word and Way* magazine reported that the Higher Learning Commission of Chicago is opening an investigation into SBU's accreditation following the destructive actions of the last two years by the Missouri Baptist Convention take over. Attempts were made to eliminate religion and philosophy professors and the Redford School of Theology. Complaints from SBU alumni led to the investigation. Should the university lose its accreditation, significant results would negatively impact the university's immediate and long range future.

Second, at the SBU regular October 20, 2020 Board of Trustees, a contentious open session led to an executive closed session. In the closed session, SBU President Dr. Eric Turner, presented his resignation to be effective on November 20, 2020. He had served in that role for just over two years. Turner, in a statement released on October 21, 2020, said, "As the University and Missouri Baptist Convention rearticulate their long-standing relationship, I think it is vital for the two entities to have a fresh start with new leadership at the helm." It was a gracious acknowledgment.

With accreditation under review and a new president selected by the fundamentalist dominated Board of Trustees, there are predictions of continued problems for the university. In the spring of 2021, there will likely be an exodus of concerned faculty and staff. It is also likely that students will react with transfers to other more academically, creditable schools. SBU alumni will have strong reactions to the changes being made with a great loss of support.

It is another indication of the hardships forced on people whose lives have been devoted to Southwest Baptist University. The dominance of fundamentalists' political control will only continue to create controversy and hardship.

Me and Fundamentalists

Authors' Publications

Paul Bass

No Little Dreams: Henry Garland Bennett: Educator and Statesman, 2007

Fellow Dreamers: Oklahoma, Education and the World, 2008

Touching the Dream: Point Four, 2009

In Jesus' Names, 2010; republished 2020

Minor Characters of the Bible, 2011; republished 2020

Robert S. Kerr: Oklahoma's Pioneer King, 2012

Me and Church, 2014; republished 2020

Grace through Tolerance, 2013; republished 2021

Leadership and Learning: History of Oklahoma State University's School of International Studies, 2016

History of Fort Leonard Wood, Missouri, 2016

Pioneer Churches of Springfield, Missouri, 2017

Missouri Innovators, 2019

Me and Fundamentalists, 2020

Bob Perry

Models of Multifamily Housing Ministry, 1989

Values-Based Tactical Planning for Religious Organizations, 1994

Pass the Power Please, 1995, reprinted 1997 and 2011

Futuropting: How Churches Can Do Multiple Scenario Planning, 1995

Congregational Wellness: Help for Broken Churches, 1997

Find a Niche and Scratch It: Marketing Your Congregation, 2003

Leadership the Ozarks Way, 2004

Me and Fundamentalists

Research and Resources

Books

Bartee, Wayne. *Greene County Baptist Churches in Ministry 1838-1984*, 1984

Follett, Ken. *A Column of Fire*. New York, New York: Viking Press, 2017, page 775

James, Rob (editor). *The Takeover in the Southern Baptist Convention: a Brief History*. SBC Today Decatur, Georgia, 1989

Kell, Carl L., Editor. *Exiled: Voices of the Southern Baptist Convention Holy War*. Knoxville: University of Tennessee Press. 2006

Shuden, Walter B., *The Struggle for the Soul of the SBC: Moderate Responses to the Fundamentalist Movement*. Mercer University Press, 1993

Youngblood, Grace M. *A Century for Christ, 1873-1973: The Story of Greene County Baptist Association*. 1973

Articles

Kaylor, Brian. "SBU, MBC Tensions Dominate MBC Meeting" *Word&Way*, November 2019

Kaylor, Brian. "President Condemns Paige Patterson" *Word&Way*, February 2020

Kaylor, Brian. "MBC Changes Nominating Rules Amid SBU Controversy" *Word and Way*, September 14, 2020

Kaylor, Brian. "Reading the Bible Like Enslavers" *Word and Way*, September 16, 2020

Other

"Cooperative Baptist Fellowship," wikipedia.org/wiki/Cooperative-Baptist-   Fellowship"

Me and Fundamentalists

Acknowledgements

The creation of this book was possible only with the help and inspiration of many people who have had a big impact on our personal and professional experiences. Some have been great teachers, but most were just great friends.

Getting the ideas for the book into a printed publication also required the help of friends and family. Jan Bass offered her usual good talents in proofreading and editing. Respected author Bob Dale was kind to offer material for the Foreword. Wayne Bartee, retired professor of European History, graciously provided needed proofreading and suggestions. We also appreciate Dr. Larry Baker, retired pastor and seminary professor and dean, for helpful suggestions and a very generous statement for the back cover.

A special thanks to Brian Kaylor, Editor and President of the *Word and Way*. He has been on the forefront of reporting on the fundamentalists' activities in Missouri. He was gracious in giving his time and attention to proofread our book and provide a generous endorsement.